CREATIVE SEWING PROJECTS
with Your
Embroidery Machine

CREATIVE SEWING PROJECTS

with Your

Embroidery Machine

Pamela J. Hastings

Sterling Publishing Co., Inc.
New York

A Sterling/Sewing Information Resources Book

A Sterling/Sewing Information Resources Book

1 3 5 7 9 10 8 6 4 2

First paperback edition published in 1998 by
Sterling Publishing Company, Inc.
387 Park Avenue South, New York, N.Y. 10016
Originally published in hardcover under the title
Creative Sewing Projects with Computerized Machines
© 1997 by Pamela J. Hastings
Distributed in Canada by Sterling Publishing
% Canadian Manda Group, One Atlantic Avenue, Suite 105
Toronto, Ontario, Canada M6K 3E7
Distributed in Great Britain and Europe by Cassell PLC
Wellington House, 125 Strand, London WC2R 0BB, England
Distributed in Australia by Capricorn Link (Australia) Pty Ltd.
P.O. Box 6651, Baulkham Hills, Business Centre, NSW 2153, Australia
Printed in China

Sterling ISBN 0-8069-8646-8

ABOUT THE AUTHOR

Pamela Hastings began sewing at the age of 12 making Christmas toys for the family pets. With the help of her high school home economics teacher, her sewing skills greatly improved and she moved on to more complex and creative projects.

After graduating from Keene State College in Keene, New Hampshire, with a degree in home economics, Pam began her career working for several companies in the home sewing industry. She has made numerous guest appearances on national and local television programs, hosted a sewing program on the Home and Garden Network as a spokesperson for Singer®, as well as appeared in, wrote, and coordinated the Butterick "Sew by Video" series.

Pam resides in Wall, New Jersey, with her husband, Geof, and sons, Christopher and Connor.

SPECIAL THANK YOU'S:

To my mother for dropping everything to baby-sit a newborn and a 3 1/2-year-old 24 hours a day so I could make my samples and attend photo shoots. To my father for driving my mother back and forth to my house every time I needed her.

And to my husband, Geof, for putting up with fabric in every room of the house and the constant background hum of several embroidery machines going at the same time.

TABLE OF CONTENTS

INTRODUCTION

About 12 years ago when I began working at Singer® Sewing Company, they were just introducing a line of sewing machines called miracle machines — the top of the line was the 6268, the first home sewing machine with built-in embroidery. It was quite a novelty and very impressive. I remember thinking at the time, that sewing machines had reached their peak and couldn't possibly advance any more.

How wrong I was! Machines have advanced by leaps and bounds since then, and as I prepared for this book, I learned that there was more to come in the embroidery area.

Ten years after the introduction of the 6268, Singer® introduced the Quantum XL-100 — a full-featured sewing machine with professional quality embroideries. New Home™, Brother®, and Husqvarna Viking® also introduced embroidery machines. Although I was more impressed than ever with what these machines could do, I kept thinking, what will sewers do with all those stitches? How many embroidered sweat shirts and napkins could someone possibly need?

JoAnn Pugh-Gannon and I met several years ago when we both began our freelance careers. With sewing machine backgrounds in common, we discussed the advances in machine technology. I told JoAnn that an ideal book for her company to produce would be one with project ideas for embroidery machine owners — projects that were enhanced by embroidery and didn't scream, "Guess what? I own an embroidery machine!"

Well, JoAnn loved the idea and decided halfway through my second pregnancy that I should write it. After the panic wore off and I began thinking of projects, I became hooked on these machines. They are such fun to use and coming up with ideas was even more fun.

In addition to my own project ideas, each sewing machine company was asked to provide projects. Samples were provided by Bernina®, Brother, Pfaff, Singer, and Husqvarna Viking. While the "company" projects are machine specific, the ideas can certainly be adapted to any machine. The purpose of this book is to provide information on embroidery machines and inspiration for all types of projects.

Chapters One and Two focus on equipment and getting started. Sewing machines, scanners, and computer capabilities are discussed, along with embroidery cards and notions. (Note: Machine features are highlighted, but visit your local dealer for complete information on each machine and any updated models.)

Chapters Three through Six provide project ideas and directions for a variety of projects. We hope our ideas will inspire you to be creative with the endless uses for embroideries.

UNDERSTANDING THE EQUIPMENT

oday's sewing equipment makes it easier and more fun than ever to create and design your own projects. Top-of-the-line machines, scanners, and computer-digitizing provide the sewer endless possibilities at the touch of a button.

SEWING MACHINES

All of the major sewing machine companies now offer machines with professional embroidery capabilities. Embroidery capabilities are either built in to the sewing machine or are available on embroidery-only machines. Pictured here are top-of-the-line sewing machines. We have highlighted some of the features of each machine to give you an idea of what they are capable of. We do recommend, however, that you review your instruction manual or visit a reputable dealer to learn how to use all the features available on your particular model.

Bernina's 1630 is a full-featured sewing machine with a wide range of stitches and capabilities. Stitches are selected using a "mouse" or command ball to place an arrow on the stitch you would like and pressing "OK". The 1630 sews motifs and monograms up to 50mm. Designs may be sewn in 16 different directions and additional design keys are available for purchase. In addition to the built-in stitch designer, Bernina offers the **Bernina Designer**, allowing you to link your sewing machine and your personal

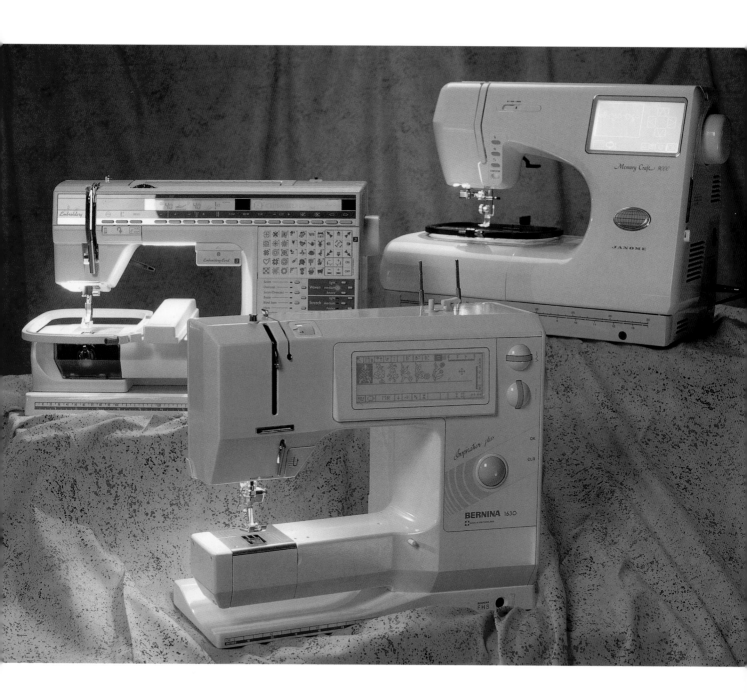

SEWING MACHINES

computer to scan designs or create your own original designs. Embroidery capabilities are available on the **Deco 600**, an embroidery-only sewing machine.

The Husqvarna Viking #1+ combines embroidery with a full range of sewing features. Stitches are selected by simply touching the picture of a desired stitch on an interchangeable cassette. Cassettes available include utility and decorative stitches and a variety of alphabets.

Professional embroideries are created by removing the main bed of the sewing machine and replacing it with an embroidery bed. An embroidery card and cassette then are inserted into the machine. Embroideries are selected in the same manner as utility stitches — by touching the picture of the desired motif. Designs may be mirror-imaged, rotated and sewn in 9 different sizes. In addition, designs may be moved within the hoop for precise placement. Each embroidery card contains 35 designs and Husqvarna Viking also has an embroidery library with thousands of motifs designed by professional embroiderers. Simply select the motifs you want and receive them from the company on an embroidery card or computer disk. Embroidery designs may even be downloaded into your computer via the Internet.

Husqvarna Viking also offers a mid-line combination embroidery/sewing machine called the **Rose**. The Rose offers 40 built-in decorative and utility stitches that are selected at the touch of a button. This machine gives the stitches the same professional quality embroidery system as the #1+.

The **Memory Craft 9000** by Janome New Home is a multi-featured sewing machine offering both traditional and embroidery capabilities. All of the sewing functions on this machine are accessible by touching the "Visual Touch Screen". This extra-large screen provides all the information you need when sewing utility or embroidery stitches.

To embroider on the Memory Craft 9000, a Memory Card is inserted into the side of the sewing machine and the embroidery hoop is attached to a carriage at the back of the machine. Designs are selected by touching a picture of the desired motif on the screen. As the design is sewn, the section that is being stitched along with the recommended

SEWING MACHINES

color of thread appears on screen. The machine automatically stops between thread changes and for broken threads or empty bobbins. New Home offers a unique "MultiCombo Embroidery" feature which allows for foolproof placement of embroideries. This feature allows several patterns to be accurately combined to create extra-large embroideries.

Pfaff's Creative 7570 offers state-of-the-art sewing machine features combined with machine embroidery. To select a stitch, a key is pressed to bring up various stitch screens. Once the desired stitch is on screen, a key directly under the stitch is pressed. The embroidery or Fantasy unit is attached to the back of the machine and Fantasy Cards are inserted in the left side of the machine near the base. After a card is inserted, the card key is pressed and motifs appear on the LCD screen. You simply scroll through the screen to locate the desired motif and press the button under the motif. Once a design has been selected, it may be enlarged or reduced, as well as rotated. Motifs from

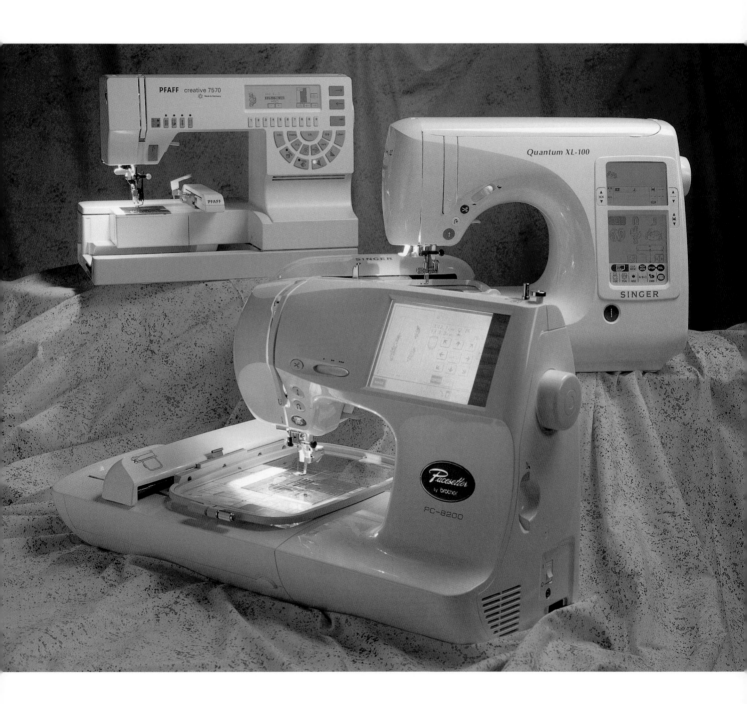

SEWING MACHINES

various cards may be combined and saved in memory and embroidered as one design. (For example, a motif may be combined with a name under it.) The 7570 stops between colors for thread changes and alerts the sewer when the bobbin is low.

Pfaff also offers the **Creative Designer** for creating your own decorative stitches, as well as PC-Designer Software which allows you to create your own stitches and embroidery motifs.

The Brother Pacesetter PC-8200 provides everything you need to enjoy fine sewing and professional embroidery. Brother's large LCD screen displays stitches, as well as sewing advice, for fuss-free sewing. In addition to utility and decorative stitches, the Pacesetter PC-8200 features "My Custom Stitch," a design package for on-screen stitch creation.

Embroidery on the PC-8200 is accomplished by replacing the sewing bed with an embroidery bed. You can select any one of the built-in embroidery designs, such as

5.1" x 7.1" monograms, or insert an embroidery card in the side of the machine for a broader selection. Embroidery motifs are selected by simply touching the motif on the LCD screen.

Designs may be rotated, mirror-imaged, and moved within the hoop; some designs may be enlarged. The machine automatically stops for thread changes, if the bobbin is empty, or if your thread breaks. The display screen also shows suggested thread color and hoop size, and estimated embroidery time, in addition to displaying which portion of the motif is being stitched. With Brother's on-screen editing system, motifs from different embroidery cards may be combined to create new embroidery motifs or pictures. These designs may be saved in one of the memory pockets in the machine.

The **Singer Quantum XL-100** combines utility and decorative stitches with embroidery. The Quantum XL-100 features a LCD screen with "Smart Touch" for error-proof sewing. Stitches are selected by first pressing a category button at the bottom of the screen, and then touching the

SEWING MACHINES

picture of the desired stitch. To sew embroideries, the main bed of the Quantum is removed and replaced with an embroidery bed. An embroidery card is inserted into the side of the sewing machine and the motif is selected by touching the embroidery button, then the picture of the desired motif. Motifs may be enlarged or reduced, and moved to a different starting location within the hoop. Designs are available in up to eight colors and may be sewn in color or in a true outline stitch (for example, sewn with a bead stitch rather than a satin stitch).

Once a design has been selected, the LCD screen displays the design along with the section of the design being stitched. The machine automatically stops for color changes and cuts the threads when the embroidery is completed. The Quantum comes with two embroidery hoops, one for standard-size embroidery and one for small areas (such as monograms on shirt cuffs).

EMBROIDERY-ONLY MACHINES

Embroidery-only machines combine the features of a professional embroidery machine with the ease of use of a home sewing machine. Rather than upgrading to an entirely separate machine, an embroidery machine may be the perfect addition to your sewing room.

As embroidery machines essentially "sew on their own" after a motif has been selected, you can sew sections of your project on one machine while utilizing the embroidery capabilities on the other!

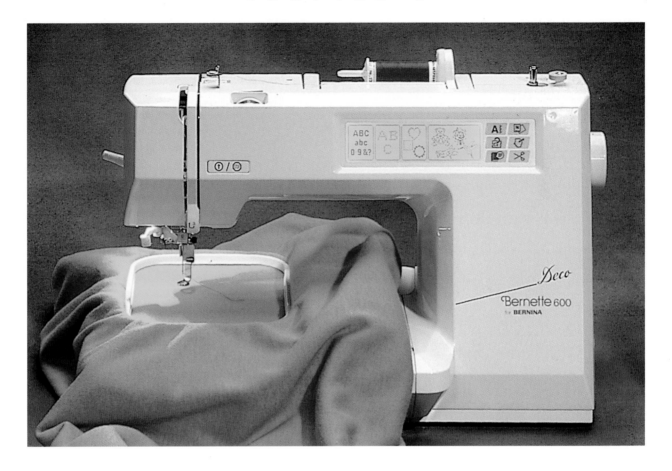

EMBROIDERY-ONLY MACHINES

The **Bernette Deco 600** from Bernina is an embroidery-only machine with 62 built-in designs (32 of which are Bernina exclusives). Additional design cards are available including Bernina "Studio" cards.

Motifs are selected by touching a picture on the LCD screen. The touch-sensitive panel displays the motif and shows which portion of the design is being sewn. Designs may be rotated and repositioned within the embroidery hoop. In addition to the standard-size hoop that comes with the Deco 600, a large hoop (4" x 6.75") and small (2.25" x 2.25") hoop are available.

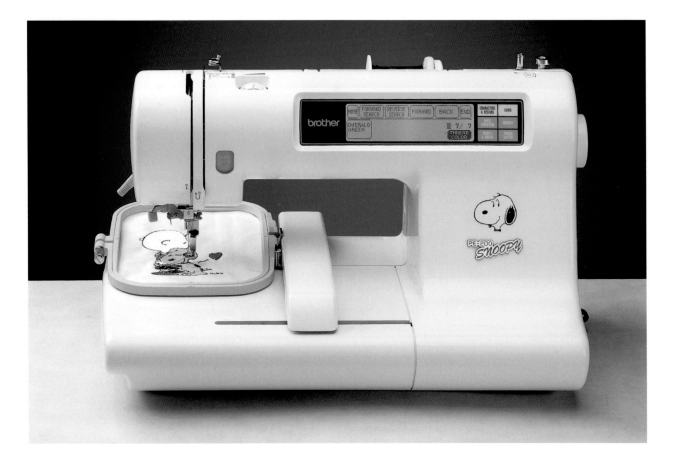

Brother's Pacesetter PE-200 offers a variety of built-in

embroidery motifs (including 45 exclusive, Snoopy licensed

designs) plus two memory cards. More than 100 frame pat-

tern combinations, nine alphabets, and 105 embroidery

motifs are built in the machine and are accessed by touch-

ing the desired motif on the LCD screen. The machine not

only stops between thread changes, and trims the thread

top and bottom, but it also has a lower thread sensor to

tell you if the bobbin thread is getting low. With a super

hoop size of 110 x 110mm, large embroideries are accom-

plished without having to reposition the hoop.

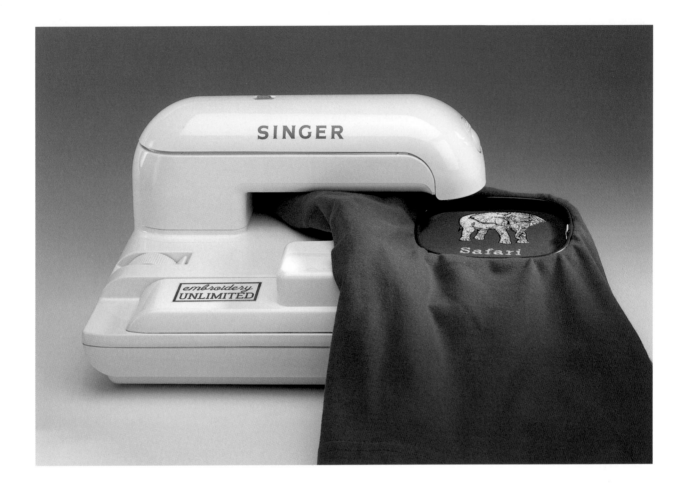

EMBROIDERY-ONLY MACHINES

Singer offers an embroidery-only machine called the **Singer Embroidery Unlimited**. This machine links with an IBM-compatible PC to produce professional-quality embroidery designs. You may choose from pre-programmed designs or lettering in four styles that are built into the software, or you may import your own designs with a scanner. Once a design has been selected or programmed, it is then stitched through the embroidery unit (your PC is hooked up directly to the sewing machine).

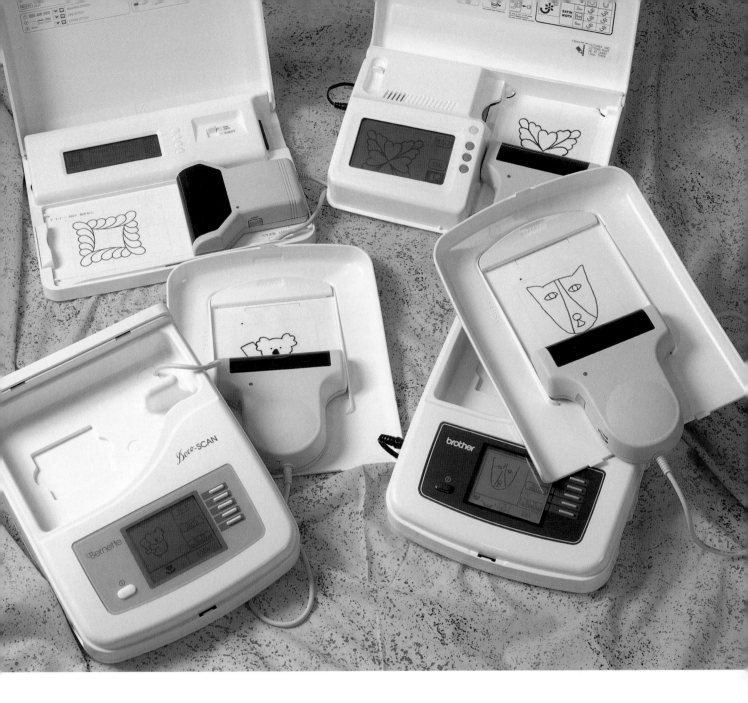

The ability to create and scan your own designs makes for unlimited embroidery ideas and capabilities. A scanner is simply a device that transforms an image into digital data that can be stored on an embroidery card and stitched out through an embroidery machine.

SCANNERS

SCANNERS

The **Memory Craft Scan 'n Sew II** by Janome New Home comes complete with preprinted design sheets ready to scan, in addition to your own creations. Designs may be scanned in as many as 12 colors and enlarged or reduced. Designs also may be embroidered in a selection of seven stitch styles.

The **Pictall** scanner from Singer has a smart screen that explains scanning procedures. Designs may be rotated as much as 360 degrees and stitched as fill-in or outline stitches. Up to 16 colors may be included in a design.

Brother's PE-SCAN and the **Bernette Deco-Scan** can reproduce designs in up to 99 colors. Designs may be enlarged to 200% or reduced by 70%. Motifs from existing embroidery cards may be imported into the scanner and edited or combined with other designs.

HOW SCANNERS WORK

The basics for operating a scanner are quite simple. Be sure to refer to your instruction manual for specifics on how to use your particular scanner and all its features.

First, the desired design is traced in black marker within the frame printed on the tracing paper provided with your scanner. A black marker is often provided.

The traced design is clipped into a guide on the scanning unit. It is then scanned, by passing the scanner over the image. The image will appear on the LCD screen. Each color in the motif is filled in individually and requires a separate scan.

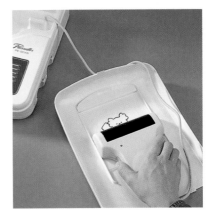

After the scanning is complete, the design is stored on an embroidery card. The embroidery card is then inserted into the sewing machine and the motif is sewn.

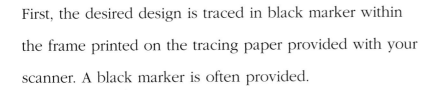

COMPUTER CAPABILITIES

In addition to scanners, computer software design packages are available for creating your own embroidery motifs.

With **Pfaff's PC-Designer Software**, you can create your own decorative stitches and embroidery motifs. The PC is directly linked to the Pfaff 7570. Designs from Creative Cards, as well as existing machine stitches, may be imported into the computer and edited. New and edited designs are saved on a blank Creative Card that has been inserted into the sewing machine.

The **Bernina Designer** links the Bernina 1630 to a personal computer for designing decorative stitches and motifs. You may draw your own designs on your computer screen or scan designs. Your new creations are then stitched out on the 1630 directly from your computer. Bernina also offers a digitizing software package for use with the Bernette Deco 600.

Husqvarna Viking and **Brother** both offer digitizing and customizing software packages. Existing embroidery cards

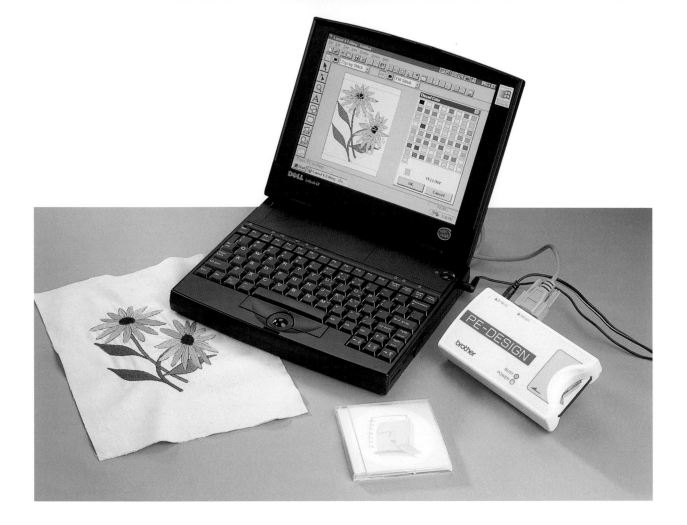

may be edited on screen or new designs may be scanned
and digitized. Color and stitch types are selected for each
portion of the embroidery. A reader/writer is attached to
the computer and a blank embroidery card is inserted into
the machine. Once a design is complete, it is stored on the
embroidery card by way of the reader/writer.

Husqvarna Viking also offers a catalog of over 4000
motifs on CD-Rom. Groups of designs may be purchased
on computer disks or an individual motif may be selected
and purchased through the Internet. After a design is purchased, it is downloaded into your computer.

ACCESSORIES

Embroidery Cards

Each company offers a number of pre-programmed embroidery cards with a variety of motifs. Embroidery cards are generally accompanied by an instruction sheet or booklet suggesting thread colors, the number of thread changes, motif sizes available, and sewing time. With the exception of the **Bernette Deco 600** and the **Brother Pacesetter**, all embroidery cards are machine specific. The Deco and Pacesetter cards are interchangeable.

Scanable Designs

Line drawings ready for scanning can be found in
ScanBooks from Brother and KanScan. ScanBooks contain
more than 50 different designs and offer scanning tips and
color suggestions.

The designs from KanScan are separated by color changes
on cards that fit most scanners. No tracing is necessary —
the scanner wand is simply passed over the design.

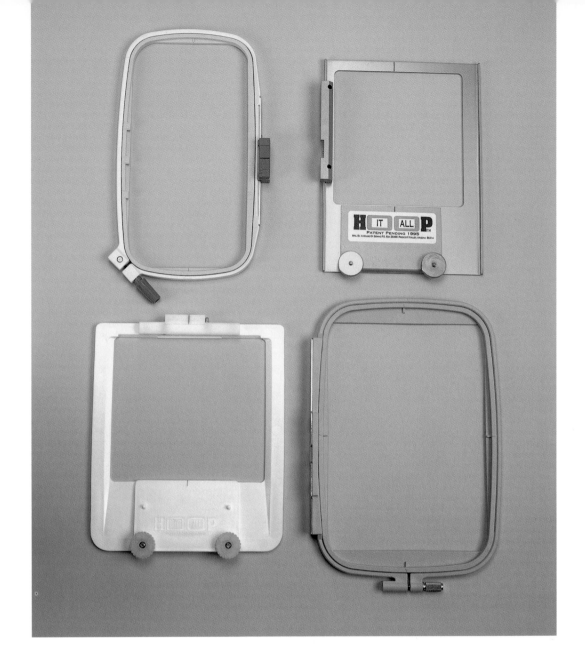

ACCESSORIES

Embroidery Hoops

In addition to the standard-size hoops that come with the embroidery machines, a variety of additional hoops are available. Larger embroidery hoops are available for the **#1+**, the **Deco 600**, and the **PE-200**. These hoops are used in conjunction with embroidery cards that produce extra-large embroidery motifs. These motifs are generally sewn in three sections, the hoop is repositioned after each section is embroidered, and the fabric stays put in the hoop. Large hoops also are very helpful when combining motifs with words. The hoop is simply repositioned with no need to remove your fabric.

The **Hoop-it-All**™ system is perfect for embroidering difficult fabrics or small areas that are difficult to hoop. This system is basically an outside hoop or base only. An adhesive stabilizer is placed, sticky side up, on the base of the hoop and fabric is "stuck" to the top side of the hoop. This system is ideal for fabrics like velvet and corduroy that may be damaged or marked in a traditional hoop. It also makes it easy to stitch hard-to-reach areas, such as on the front of a hat or on a ready-made garment.

AUTHOR'S NOTE: *The information in this chapter is meant to only inform the reader about the capabilities of embroidery machines. For specifics on your particular brand of machine or for additional information on computer capabilities, please refer to your instruction manual or consult a reputable sewing machine dealer.*

BEFORE YOU BEGIN

*T*he first step in creating

a beautifully embroidered project is

selecting the perfect motif. However,

before stitching, it is very important

to place your fabric in the hoop

correctly, select a thread that will

enhance the motif, and use the

correct stabilizer for your fabric and

entire project.

NOTIONS

THREADS

A wide variety of threads are now available for use with embroidery machines. The most popular thread is rayon. Rayon's shine and rich colors make it very suitable for embroidery designs.

Rayon is available is a variety of weights and deniers. Weight and denier actually determine the thickness of a thread. If you are sewing a very small motif, a thinner or lower density thread is most desirable. A motif that has been enlarged will most likely be enhanced by a slightly thicker thread, filling in the motif more densely.

In general, the higher the thread-weight number, the thinner the thread (for example, a 40-weight rayon is a thinner thread than a 30-weight rayon). Weights do vary from manufacturer to manufacturer so it is also important to look at the thread's denier to be sure you are getting the exact density you want. The higher the denier number of a thread, the heavier or thicker the thread is. A 30-weight thread of 180 denier will be thicker than a 30-weight thread of 175 denier.

Rayon thread is also available in solid and variegated colors and in a color twist selection (two separate threads twisted together) for embroidery use.

NOTIONS

Additional threads available for machine embroidery:

■ Metallic thread adds glitter and shine to embroideries. Like rayon thread, metallics are available in several weights and a wide range of colors.

■ Sliver® is a type of metallic thread that resembles very fine tinsel. It has a smooth, shiny appearance.

■ Cotton thread is available in a wide range of colors and gives embroidered motifs a softer look with its smooth, matte finish.

■ Lightweight yarn called Luny adds texture to motifs. Both Luny and cotton are a bit denser than rayon and fill in motifs beautifully.

Bobbin threads are generally finer and do not show on the front of your embroidery piece. The fine nature of these bobbin threads reduces the bulk on the back of embroideries. Also, the bobbin will hold more of this type of thread reducing the number of times you need to wind a new bobbin.

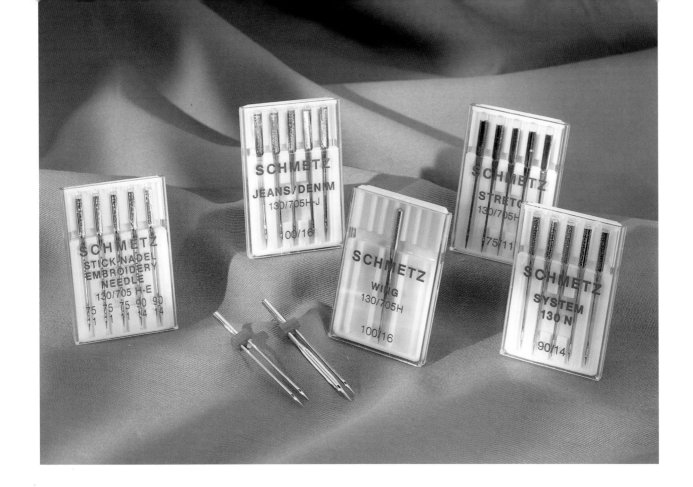

NEEDLES

It is important to change needles often when embroidering by machine. A needle that is dull or bent or has a burr will strip and fray the threads while embroidering. If you are having a problem with breaking threads, try inserting a new needle.

Size #80/12 needles are appropriate for most embroidery projects. To achieve maximum results when sewing with metallic threads, use a needle specifically designed for sewing with this type of thread.

STABILIZERS

When embroidering, it is important to back your fabric with a stabilizer. Stabilizers give fabrics added support so they do not stretch or pucker during the stitching. For best results, select the stabilizer that is most suited to your project. More than one type of stabilizer may be used.

Tear-away stabilizers perform exactly as the name implies, they tear away after stitching. Available in a variety of weights, tear-away stabilizers are suitable for most embroidery projects. Heavier versions can sometimes distort your motif when they are removed. If that happens, try using several layers of a perforated or lighweight stabilizer that tears away more easily.

Water-soluble stabilizers are transparent, plastic-like stabilizers that dissolve in water. They are perfect when working on napped fabrics, such as terrycloth or velvet. Placed on the top of the area to be embroidered, they give your embroidery a smooth appearance and prevent the loops of the towel from poking through. This stabilizer can be torn-away from the outer edges of the motif, then a quick rinse in water will remove all the remaining stabilizer.

NOTIONS

41

NOTIONS

Totally Stable™ is an iron-on, tear-away stabilizer. It temporarily fuses to any fabric and eliminates any shifting and puckering. After stitching, this stabilizer is easily torn away. Heat-Away™ is a heat-sensitive, woven fabric that disintegrates with a hot iron. It is perfect for creating cutwork appliques. After stitching, the stabilizer is heated with a hot iron and then brushed away.

Adhesive-backed, tear-away stabilizers are used to stabilize a fabric without placing it between inner and outer hoops. It adheres to the back of the embroidery hoop or Hoop-it-All, and the fabric is then finger-pressed onto the adhesive. After stitching, the stabilizer is easily removed.

Cut-away stabilizers give added permanent support to embroideries and are commonly used with sweater knits to prevent stretching and distortion. After stitching, the excess stabilizer is trimmed away.

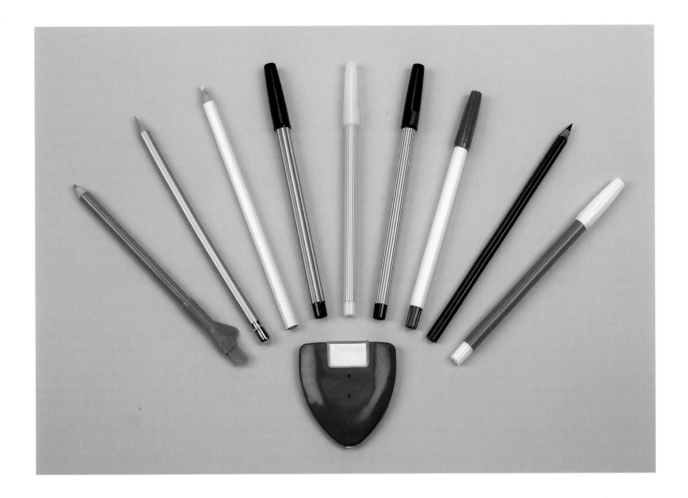

MARKING PENS

It is essential to mark the placement of your embroidery design on the fabric before placing the fabric in the hoop. A variety of marking tools are available for use on any fabric. Before using any marking tool, it is a good idea to test the marker on a scrap of fabric to see if the marks can be removed easily.

Water-soluble and air-soluble markers are two of the most popular markers available. Markings made with water-soluble pens are easily removed with cold water.

CHAPTER 2

NOTIONS

Air-soluble or disappearing markers vanish in 24 - 48 hours. If any marks remain, they may be removed with a commercial spot lifter.

Dressmaker's pencils and chalk are used when working with dark fabrics. Marks may be brushed away easily or removed with a damp cloth.

Silver marking pencils can be used on light or dark fabric, and the marks are removed by rubbing lightly with a damp cloth or by brushing lightly.

Template markers are used to trace embroidery motifs onto the mylar or plastic template and are included with your embroidery machine. These tracings are removed easily with soap and water.

DESIGN PLACEMENT

MAKING A TEMPLATE

To ensure perfect placement of an embroidery motif on your garment, it is a good idea to stitch a test sample and make a template first. Templates may be made by simply tracing a design onto the plastic template grid, or you can make your own template.

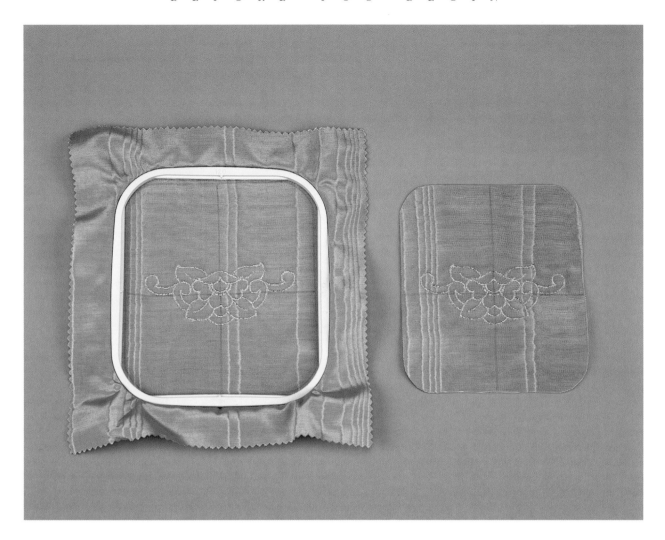

To make your own template, first embroider the desired

motif (it's not necessary to make color changes when

stitching a motif for a template). Before removing the

hoop, trace the inside edge onto the embroidered fabric

and draw a horizontal and vertical line to correspond with

the markings along the edges of the hoop. Remove the

fabric from the hoop and cut out along the traced line. Use

the horizontal and vertical markings to mark the placement

of the motif on your final project.

DESIGN PLACEMENT

EMBROIDERY ON A READY-MADE GARMENT

Embroidery on ready-to-wear may be done several ways. If the embroidery will be done in a large area that easily fits into the hoop, simply use a template to mark placement, back the garment with a suitable stabilizer, place it in a hoop, and stitch your motif.

To embroider a smaller area, such as a cuff, first mark the placement of the embroidery. Using an adhesive-backed stabilizer, placed the stabilizer's sticky side up on the bottom of your embroidery hoop or Hoop-it-All. Press the cuff onto the stabilizer, lining up the placement lines with the markings on the hoop. Attach the hoop to the machine and stitch.

To embroider a patch pocket, remove the pocket from the garment and follow the same procedure as for cuffs. Replace the pocket when your embroidery is complete.

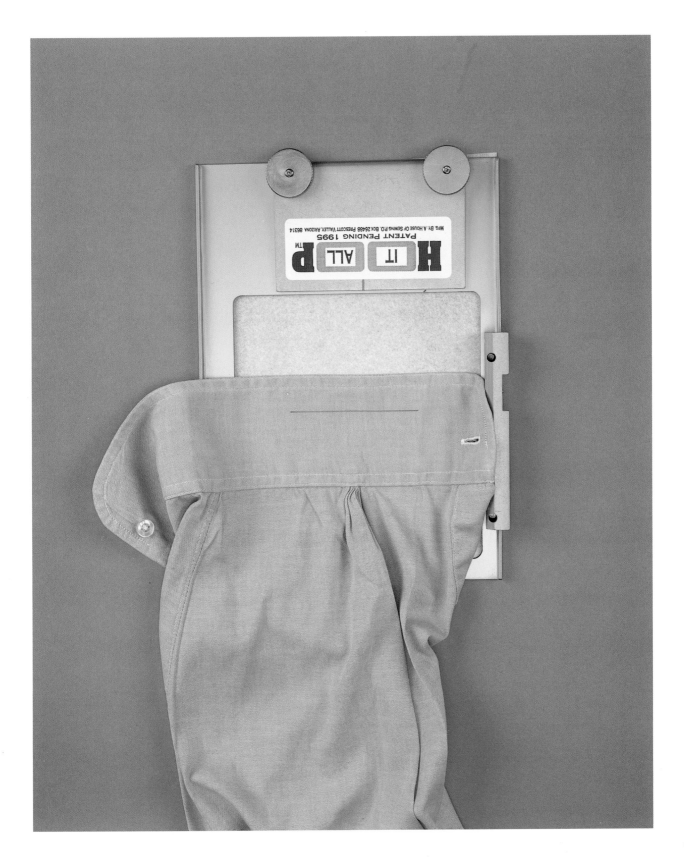

DESIGN PLACEMENT

EMBROIDERY ON A GARMENT IN PROGRESS

When constructing a garment of your own, it is easier to first embroider the fabric and then cut out the pattern piece. The correct placement for the embroidery design is easily accomplished and you are able to work with a large enough piece of fabric that easily fits into the hoop.

Begin by cutting a piece of fabric several inches longer and wider than the pattern piece. Mark the horizontal and vertical placement lines in the center of the fabric, back with stabilizer, and place in the embroidery hoop.

Center the pattern piece over the finished embroidery and cut out the piece. If the pattern piece states "Place On Fold," align the center of the embroidery under the foldline on the pattern piece and trace the pattern piece on the fabric. Then, flip the pattern piece over to trace the other half on the fabric.

HOLIDAYS AND SPECIAL OCCASIONS

nhance projects made for the holidays and special occasions by embellishing them with an appropriate embroidery. Personalize Christmas items, create your own invitations, and make a beautiful pillow to announce the birth of a new baby. Festive table accessories add just the right touch to your holiday table and an embroidered photo album is the perfect place for treasured wedding photos.

PERSONALIZED CHRISTMAS TREE SKIRT

- Butterick #4603 or appropriate pattern
- Dressmaker's pencil
- Tear-away stabilizer

- Fabric and braid as required on pattern
- Gold metallic thread
- Rayon thread in holiday colors

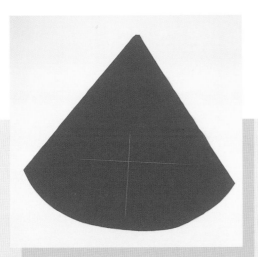

1. Cut out tree skirt according to pattern directions. Mark placement of name on each gore using a dressmaker's pencil.

2. Program the desired name into your embroidery machine following the procedure in your instruction manual. Place stabilizer behind fabric; place fabric in hoop matching placement lines with markings on hoop and embroider each name.

3. When names are complete, use a template to mark the placement of the holiday motifs. Select the desired motif, stabilize and hoop fabric, and stitch motif with rayon thread.

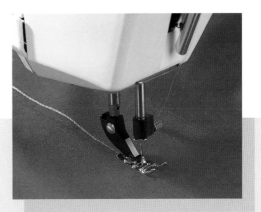

4. Finish constructing the tree skirt according to pattern directions. Before applying braid, stitch a row of decorative or satin stitches along the seamlines of the gores. Apply braid and complete as instructed in the pattern.

Mantel Scarf

YOU WILL NEED:

- Butterick #4603 (modified slightly) or appropriate pattern
- Fabric, lining and braid as required on pattern
- Water-soluble marker
- Adhesive-backed stabilizer
- Rayon thread in holiday colors
- Gold metallic thread
- 4 gold tassels
- Needle and thread

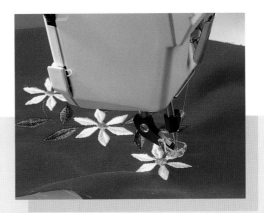

1. After cutting out the pattern, mark horizontal and vertical placement lines on your fabric. (Note: When using velvet, mark placement lines on the wrong side of the fabric as markings are often difficult to remove from velvet.) Place adhesive-backed stabilizer, sticky side up, on the underside of your embroidery hoop. Draw horizontal and vertical placement lines on the stabilizer.

2. Press wrong side of velvet onto the stabilizer matching the marked lines. Select and embroider the motif using colors of choice. Repeat with remaining sections of mantel scarf. (Note: Our mantel scarf has three sections. A candle motif was selected for the center and poinsettias for each outer section. When embroidering the poinsettias, we mirror-imaged the embroidery on the right section so the motifs would both face away from the center.)

3. Stitch decorative braid over the seam-lines of each section. Complete mantel scarf according to pattern directions. Hand-stitch tassels in place at the base of the decorative trim and at each end of the mantel scarf.

CHRISTMAS STOCKING

YOU WILL NEED:

- Stocking pattern with a cuff
- Velvet and satin as required on pattern
- Iron-on stabilizer
- 8" x 8" remnant of satin
- Rayon thread
- Disappearing marker

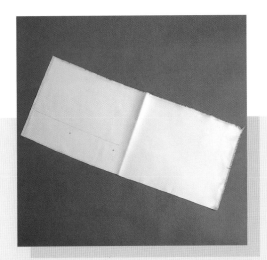

1. Cut stocking from velvet; cuff from satin. Place stabilized satin remnant in embroidery hoop and stitch desired motif. Trim embroidered fabric to a 4 1/2" x 4 1/2" diamond shape. Turn under 1/4" on all edges and press. Center motif on stocking front and stitch close to edges with decorative embroidery stitch of your choice. With right sides together, stitch stocking front to stocking back.

2. Mark placement line for name on cuff as shown. Remember the name must be stitched in the upper-right-hand section of the cuff. Stabilize fabric and place in hoop. Program and embroider name with rayon thread in color of choice.

3. To complete cuff, stitch along short edge with right sides together. Fold cuff in half, wrong sides together, and baste along raw edge. Stitch completed cuff to stocking top by placing the cuff inside the stocking with the right side of the cuff facing the wrong side of the stocking. Stitch along top edge and turn cuff to outside.

*B*ABY *B*IB

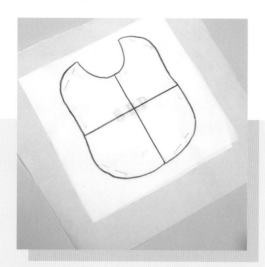

1. Trace pattern (page 122) onto tracing paper. Mark horizontal and vertical lines in center of one of the batiste pieces. Embroider desired initials in center of marked, stabilized fabric. Place pattern over layered embroidered and plain fabrics. Cut out bib.

2. Pin pre-gathered lace to edge of bib and baste in place. With right sides together, stitch bib front to bib back leaving the top edge open. Turn right side out and press.

3. Encase top edge of bib with bias tape. Pin in place. Stitch close to folded edges of bias tape.

YOU WILL NEED:

- Tracing paper
- 2 - 10" x 10" pieces of batiste
- Water-soluble marker
- Cotton embroidery thread
- Iron-on stabilizer
- 3/4 yard of pre-gathered 1/2" lace
- 24" strip of double-fold bias tape to match batiste

$\mathcal{B}$ABY $\mathcal{P}$ILLOW

(PHOTO ON PAGE 59)

1. Program the desired name into the embroidery machine. Be sure to refer to your instruction manual for the correct programming and placement procedure for your machine.

2. Mark the placement line for the name in the center of the 10" x 15" piece of batiste. Fuse stabilizer to back of fabric. Secure in hoop and embroider the name.

YOU WILL NEED:

- 1 - 10" x 15" piece of batiste and 2 - 10" x 10" pieces of batiste.
- Water-soluble marker

- Iron-on stabilizer
- Cotton embroidery thread
- 1 3/4 yards of 2" pre-gathered lace

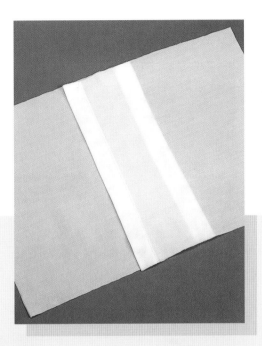

3. Pin the lace to the edges of the pillow front, keeping straight edge of lace even with the raw edge of the fabric. Machine baste in place.

4. To construct pillow back, serge along edge of each fabric piece. Turn under 1" on serged edge and stitch close to serging. Overlap finished edges of back by 3" and baste edges. Stitch pillow front and back with right sides together.

BRIDAL ALBUM COVER

(SINGER SEWING COMPANY)

YOU WILL NEED:

- 1 1/2 yards of satin or taffeta
- Three-ring binder
- Water-soluble marker
- Rayon thread
- Tear-away stabilizer
- 1 yard fusible batting

1. Cut two pieces of fabric the dimensions of binder plus 1". Cut two pieces the height of binder plus 1" x 5". Fold one large piece of fabric in half crosswise and press. Embroider a floral motif in center of right half of fabric for front cover. Mark placement line for lettering; stabilize and stitch "Our Wedding".

2. Embellish outer edge of album cover with "Leaf & Vine" stitch. For correct placement of decorative stitches, first stitch the design on a scrap of fabric. Place this swatch on the album cover to determine where to begin stitching. Fuse batting to wrong side of album front.

3. To create the eyelet trim, sew scallops along a 3" x 60" strip of fabric. Center eyelet stitches on every other scallop. Punch out eyelets using an eyelet punch and trim scalloped edge. Finish the short edges of the eyelet trim with a 1/4 double-fold hem. Gather trim to a 34" strip and baste to album front.

4. To complete the cover, finish off one long edge of each small piece of fabric. Baste one finished flap to each end of the cover lining along the raw edges. Stitch cover front and lining, right sides together, leaving an opening for turning. Turn right side out and slipstitch opening closed.

Silver Server

(PFAFF)

YOU WILL NEED:

- 21 1/2"-diameter paper circle
- 30" x 30" piece of decorator fabric
- Disappearing marker
- Tear-away stabilizer
- Pfaff Creative Fantasy Card #7 or appropriate design
- Gold metallic thread
- 5 1/2" x 2 1/2" remnant of gold lamé
- Filler cord

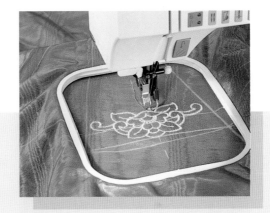

1. Trace the 21 1/2" circle onto your fabric with a disappearing marker. Divide the circle into 12 pie-shaped sections. Enlarge on a photocopier the silver server pattern shown on page 124 and transfer the marking onto six of the 12 sections.

2. Back fabric with stabilizer and place one of six marked sections in embroidery hoop. Be sure to line up the vertical line with vertical markings on hoop and center horizontal hoop markings between the two horizontal lines. Insert Creative Fantasy Card and select frame 3/4. Use key #1 or #2 to select motif, rotate design 270°. Embroider the motif and repeat the procedure in the remaining five sections.

3. To complete the silver server, fold circle in half with embroideries facing you. Mark center of the fabric at fold. Open out fabric and stitch an additional motif where marked. Trim away center of this motif and back with gold lamé. Fold fabric in half, wrong sides together. Using a satin stitch, sew along marked lines over filler cord. Trim excess fabric from edges of motifs.

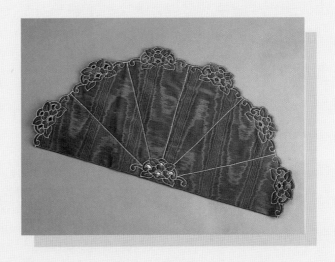

Table Runner

(PFAFF)

(PHOTO ON PAGE 64)

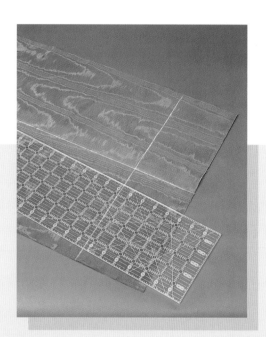

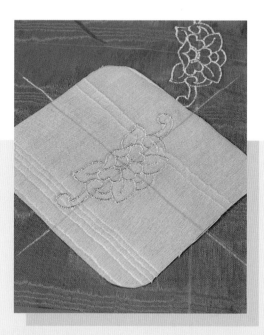

1. Draw a vertical line in the center of each end of the table runner fabric. Draw a horizontal line approximately 5" from the short edge of the fabric piece. Back fabric with stabilizer and place fabric in embroidery hoop matching marked lines with lines on hoop. Stitch motif from card using gold metallic thread.

2. Make a template of the motif to use for correct placement of additional motifs. Determine the position of the next motif by laying the template on the fabric. Mark the placement after desired position is achieved.

YOU WILL NEED:

- 48" x 18" piece of decorator fabric
- Disappearing marker
- Tear-away stabilizer
- Gold metallic thread

- Pfaff Creative Fantasy Card #7 or appropriate design
- 2 yards of filler cord
- Seam sealant

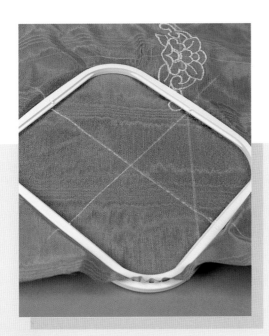

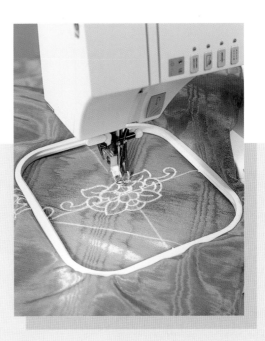

3. Remove the template and connect markings. Stabilize the fabric and place in embroidery hoop. Line up new lines with marks on embroidery hoop.

4. Embroider remaining motifs on table runner. Finish long edges of table runner by drawing a straight line along each edge. Using a narrow satin stitch, stitch along marked line over filler cord. Place seam sealant around all edges and motifs; trim close to stitching.

GREETING CARDS

YOU WILL NEED:

- Card stock or heavy paper
- Cotton embroidery thread
- Solid fabric remnants for embroidery

- Water-soluble marker
- Tear-away stabilizer
- Paper-backed fusible web
- Printed fabric remnants for outside of card

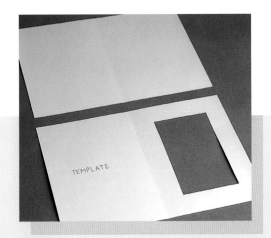

1. Enlarge or reduce the card template (page 123) to the desired size. Cut out one pattern from card stock (to be used for the finished card) and cut a second pattern for a template. Cut out the front section of the card on the template only.

2. Back solid fabric with stabilizer, and embroider desired motif. Remove stabilizer and press fusible web onto back of fabric. Center the embroidery in the "window" of the template and trace the outer edge of the card front. Cut along traced line and remove the paper backing from the fusible web.

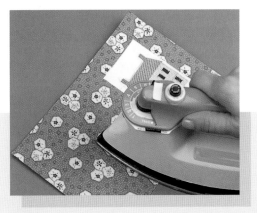

3. Fuse paper-backed web to the wrong side of the printed fabric remnant. Trace template onto fabric and cut out pattern. Front "window" also will need to be cut out. Remove the paper backing from the fusible web.

4. Fuse embroidery motif onto the front of the card. Next, center the "window" of the printed fabric over the embroidery motif and fuse in place.

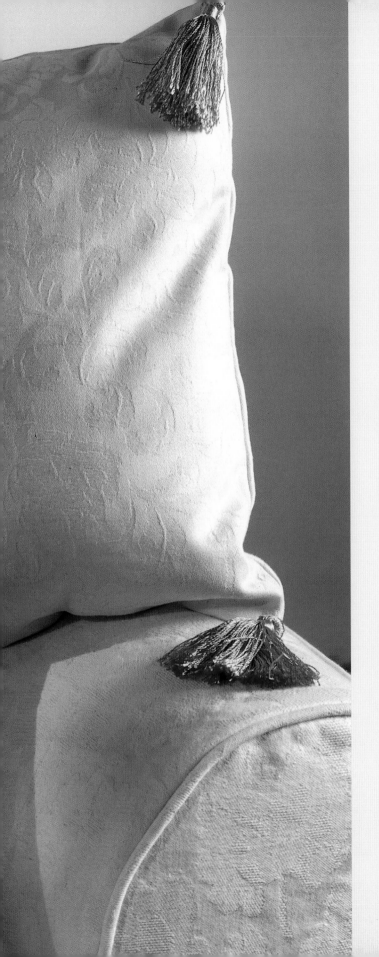

HOME DECORATING

ecorative stitches and
motifs can add just the right touch to
everything from lampshades and
table toppers to picture frames and
pillows. The possibilities for
enhancing home decorating projects
are endless. Use motifs as an accent
on valances and window shades, or
find motifs that create a theme for a
project, like our Peter Rabbit Valance.

SHAPED VALANCE

YOU WILL NEED:

- Fabric and lining as required on pattern
- Template marker
- Template grid and black marker
- Butterick pattern #5946 or appropriate pattern
- Water-soluble marker
- Tear-away stabilizer
- Rayon thread to match cord
- Optional: decorative braid

1. Stitch a sample motif on a scrap of your fabric. Note how design is stitched out, as you may need to rotate design when stitching the embroidery on your valance. Trace completed embroidery onto the template grid with a black marker. Cut out according to directions.

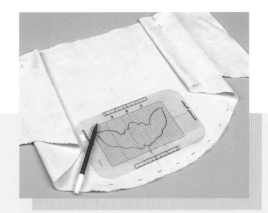

2. Pin-baste pleats in top of valance and mark the seam allowance at the bottom edge of the valance using the water-soluble marker. Draw a vertical line in the center of the scalloped section. Place the center of motif on vertical line the desired distance from the bottom of the valance. (We flipped our template over, since the motif will be mirror-imaged when stitched.)

3. Stabilize and hoop fabric, matching marked lines with markings on the hoop. Select motif, mirror-image, and stitch. Remove fabric from hoop and tear away the stabilizer.

4. Stitch decorative braid along bottom edge of valance, keeping edge of braid even with the raw edge of the valance. Complete valance according to pattern directions.

Fabric Shade

- Fusible shade backing
- Decorator fabric (refer to directions with shade backing for fabric requirements)
- Water-soluble marker
- Rayon or cotton embroidery thread
- Seam sealant
- Embroidery scissors
- Roller for shade

1. Fuse shade backing to fabric as directed. Turn up 3" hem along bottom edge. Mark placement line for decorative stitching on the front of the shade with a water-soluble marker. Select desired decorative stitch and thread, and sew along marked line. If you are using an extra-wide decorative stitch, keep presser foot parallel to marked lines and hem.

2. Place a small amount of seam sealant along the bottom of edge of the decorative stitching. Allow seam sealant to dry thoroughly and trim close to stitching with embroidery scissors.

3. Trim shade to finished width as directed on shade backing instructions. Attach completed shade to roller using a staple gun. Add valance or additional window treatment of choice.

Cutwork Pillow

YOU WILL NEED:

- 2 - 17" x 17" decorator fabric (for one 16" pillow)
- Water-soluble marker
- Iron-on stabilizer
- Rayon thread
- Seam sealant
- 17" x 17" fabric for underlay
- 4 tassels
- 16" pillow form
- Needle and thread

1. Mark horizontal and vertical lines on the right side of one decorator fabric square. Stabilize and hoop fabric. Stitch desired cutwork motif. Put seam sealant on inside edges of design and trim away inside fabric.

2. Place right side of contrasting fabric to wrong side of embroidered fabric. Baste around outer edges of fabric.

3. Baste tassels in corners of pillow front. With right sides together, stitch pillow front to pillow back, leaving an opening for turning. Turn pillow right side out, insert pillow form, and slipstitch opening closed with a needle and thread.

PERSONALIZED FLANGE PILLOW

YOU WILL NEED:

- Tear-away stabilizer
- Rayon thread
- 2 - 15" x 12" pieces of linen
- 1 - 11" x 30" strip of contrasting fabric
- Water-soluble marker
- 3 - 1" buttons
- 14" pillow form

1. Back linen with stabilizer and stitch desired letter on the right side of one linen piece. Note the 12" edges of fabric are the top and bottom of pillow. With right sides together, stitch front to back, leaving left side open. Trim corners and turn

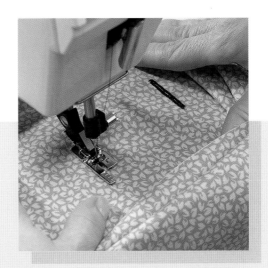

2. To construct flange, stitch fabric strip, right sides together, along short end. Press seam open. Fold fabric, wrong sides together, keeping raw edges even. Mark buttonhole placement on front of flange and stitch buttonholes.

3. Stitch flange to pillow, buttonhole side of flange to embroidered side of pillow. Sew buttons to inside opposite buttonholes. Insert pillow form and button closed.

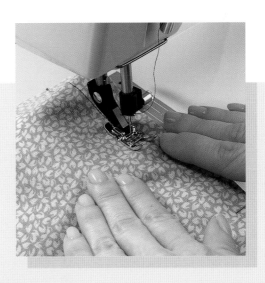

Seaside Pillow

- Iron-on stabilizer
- Rayon thread
- 1 - 10" x 10" square of solid fabric
- 2 - 17" x 17" squares of fabric (for one 16" pillow)
- 1 1/2 yards of decorative braid
- 2 yards of brush fringe
- 1 - 16" pillow form
- Needle and thread

1. Fuse 10" square of fabric with stabilizer and embroider fish motif in center. Trim square to 8" and baste in center of pillow front. Center braid over raw edge of inset and stitch in place.

2. Baste brush fringe to pillow front keeping edge of fringe even with raw edge of pillow. Stitch pillow front to pillow back, right sides together, leaving an opening for turning. Turn right side out, insert pillow form, and slip-stitch opening closed with a needle and thread.

PETER RABBIT VALANCE

YOU WILL NEED:

- Medium-weight, non-woven fusible interfacing
- 8 pieces of white fabric, at least 10" x 10"
- Rayon thread in a variety of colors
- Ruler
- Water-soluble marker
- 6 - 5 1/2" x 5 1/2" peach fabric (for 36" window)
- 3 - 5 1/2" x 5 1/2" squares of blue fabric
- 2 - 29" x 3" strips of blue fabric
- 1 - 42" x 3" strip of blue fabric
- Rotary cutter and mat
- Triangle of lining fabric - 42" x 32" x 32"

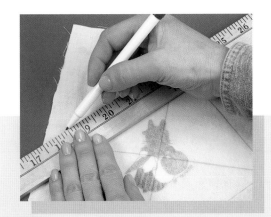

1. Fuse interfacing to wrong side of white fabric squares and embroider desired motif in center of each square. Make a 5 1/2" square template from stabilizer and draw an "X" in the center. Center template over embroidery and trace outer edge; trim along marked lines.

2. Alternating colored squares and embroidered squares, stitch fabric squares together creating triangular shape matching template shown on page 124. Stitch border strips to sides of valance.

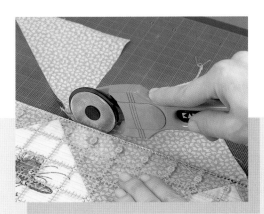

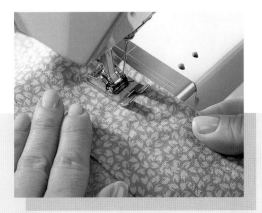

3. Using a rotary cutter, mat and ruler, trim the top edge of the valance, creating a straight edge (top half of each square will be trimmed away). Stitch remaining border strip to top edge of valance.

4. Stitch lining to valance, rights sides together, leaving an opening in one side for turning. Do not stitch through the edges of the top border — this will be the opening for your curtain rod. To form casing, sew two rows of straight stitching 1 1/2" apart in top border.

Heirloom Pillow

(HUSQVARNA VIKING)

Vogue Patterns 9530, Photography by Tom McCavera

YOU WILL NEED:

- Vogue #7955 or appropriate pattern
- Fabric as required on pattern
- Water-soluble marker
- Iron-on stabilizer
- Husqvarna Viking embroidery cassette #9 or appropriate design
- 30-weight rayon thread
- 40-weight rayon thread
- Pillow form

1. Fold pillow front in half to find center. Draw vertical and horizontal lines in center of pillow. Next, draw diagonal lines from corner to corner across the center of pillow front. Fuse stabilizer to wrong side of pillow front.

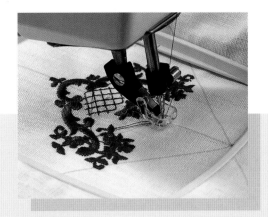

2. Hoop fabric on the vertical line so the center of the embroidery hoop is 3" from the center of the pillow. Insert cassette and select stitch #33. Increase length and width to 4.5mm. Stitch motif using 30-weight rayon in color of choice.

3. Repeat the embroidery procedure in step 2 on each horizontal and vertical line. Tip: When sewing a multi-colored embroidery in just one color, press the "stop" button before you begin to sew. This will allow the machine to stitch the entire embroidery without stopping for programmed color changes.

4. Place fabric in hoop on diagonal line with hoop center 4 1/4" from fabric center. Forward to and stitch color #6. Repeat on each diagonal. For center motif, place hoop in center front; stitch color #6 in smallest size using 40-weight thread. Rotate motif twice, then stitch. Complete pillow as directed.

Lampshade

(PFAFF)

YOU WILL NEED:

- Purchased lamp and paper shade
- Freezer paper
- Masking tape
- 3/4 yard of 60" wide fabric (may vary depending on size of lamp shade)
- Water-soluble marker
- Pfaff Creative Fantasy Card #7 or appropriate design
- Tear-away stabilizer
- Rayon thread
- Ruler
- Pearl cotton to match the thread
- Seam sealant
- Paper-backed fusible web
- Double-stick tape

1. Tape straight edge of freezer wrap to seam of shade. Wrap paper around shade overlapping seams. Tape the end. Cut the excess paper from the top and bottom of the shade. Remove pattern from the shade.

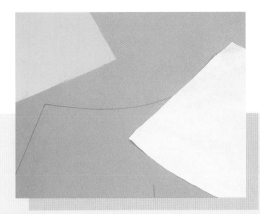

2. Place wrong side of pattern to right side of fabric and trace around outer edge. Make a template of your motif and mark placement lines of each motif.

3. Insert Creative Fantasy Card #7 and select screen #2/4. Program stitch by pressing key #5 or #6. Change pattern size to 107/57mm. Stabilize and hoop fabric, and attach embroidery hoop to machine. Move design as far to the right as possible and stitch. Without removing the hoop, mirror-image the design and move it as far to the left as possible; stitch motif.

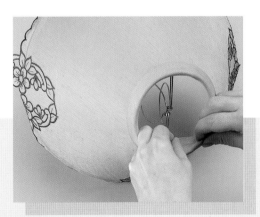

4. To finish, draw line connecting each motif 1/4" down from bottom line. Stitch scallop stitch over pearl cotton along line. Apply seam sealant to all edges; trim. Add paper-backed fusible web to wrong side of fabric. Cut bias strip of fabric 2 1/2" wide by circumference of shade top plus 1/2". Stitch to top. Fuse fabric over shade. Turn bias strip to inside; secure with double-stick tape.

PICTURE FRAME

(PFAFF)

YOU WILL NEED:

- Pfaff Creative Fantasy Card #7 or appropriate design
- Rayon thread
- 12" square of decorator fabric
- Disappearing marker
- Tear-away stabilizer
- Seam sealant
- Self-stick frame pattern

1. Make a template of your design. Program desired motif and rotate to the position you will use for your frame. Stitch motif. Before removing fabric from the hoop, mark vertical and horizontal lines, and trace the inner edge of the hoop. Remove hoop and trim along traced line.

2. Place picture frame pattern on the right side of your fabric and trace the inner and outer edges. Place template in desired location on picture frame pattern and mark vertical and horizontal placement lines.

3. Stabilize fabric and place in embroidery hoop, matching placement lines to lines on the hoop. Stitch motif. Apply seam sealant to the portion of the embroidery that is inside the picture frame and trim. Complete picture frame according to manufacturer's directions.

EMBROIDERED TABLE TOPPER

(PFAFF)

YOU WILL NEED:

- 45" x 45" square of decorator fabric
- Disappearing marker
- Pfaff Creative Fantasy Card #7 or appropriate design
- Tear-away stabilizer
- Rayon thread
- Pearl cotton to match rayon
- Seam sealant

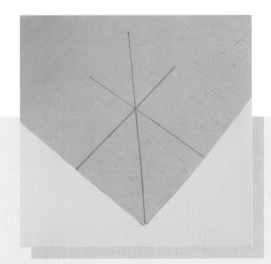

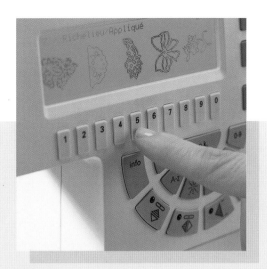

1. At corner of fabric, mark a line 2" from the edge at each side. The lines should intersect at the corner. Draw a line on the bias intersecting the center of the previous lines. This is the placement line for centering the hoop.

2. Insert Creative Fantasy Card #7 into machine and select screen #2/4. Press key #5 to select motif. Change the motif size to 107/57mm and move motif as far to right as possible. Stabilize and hoop the fabric matching bias line with vertical markings on hoop; stitch motif, mirror-image, and stitch a second motif.

3. To complete the table topper, draw a straight line along each edge connecting motifs. Select a scallop or satin stitch and stitch along the marked lines over pearl cotton. Apply seam sealant to all edges, let dry, and trim close to stitching.

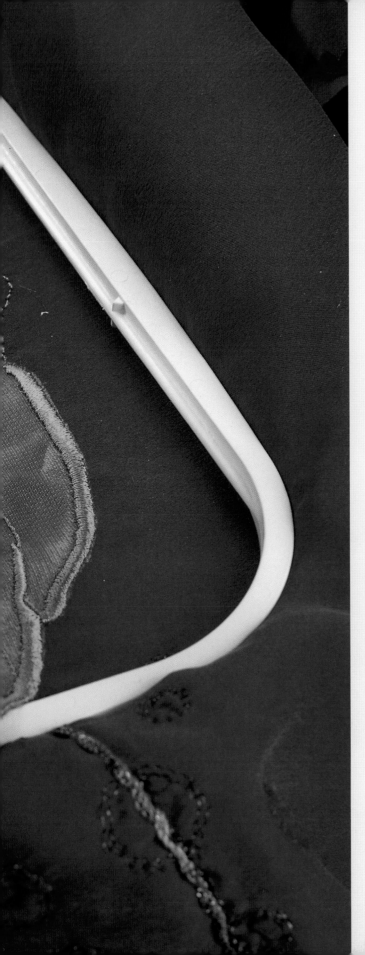

GARMENTS AND ACCESSORIES

*G*arments and accessories can be accented with an elegant monogram or motif to add just the right touch. Or create something more elaborate by combining motifs and decorative stitches to create your own wearable works of art.

PICKET FENCE DRESS

(HUSQVARNA VIKING)

YOU WILL NEED:

- Jumper pattern or appropriate dress or skirt pattern
- Solid blue fabric as required on pattern
- Tear-away stabilizer
- Disappearing marker
- Rayon thread
- Green fabric for bottom of jumper
- Organza
- Adhesive-backed stabilizer
- Seam sealant

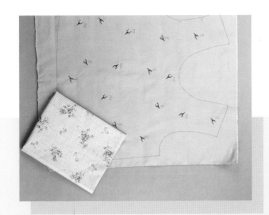

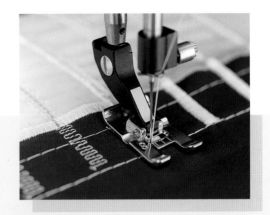

1. Trace bodice front onto fabric and mark placement of rosebuds. Using tear-away stabilizer, embroider rose buds at markings. Note: It is not necessary to remove hoop to stitch each bud. Using the large embroidery hoop, move and rotate the motif to each marking within the hoop.

2. Satin-stitch the bottom edge of skirt on blue fabric and top edge of green fabric. Place blue and green fabrics 5" apart; baste to a piece of stabilized organza. Mark placement line for fence and stitch along lines with a multi-stitch zigzag. Stitch each picket with satin stitch, tapering to a point.

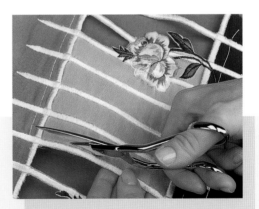

3. Mark placement of roses along fence. Place adhesive-backed stabilizer, sticky side up, on bottom of embroidery hoop. Press fabric into hoop, centering markings. Select rose motif and stitch roses along fence.

4. Apply seam sealant to edges of fence and roses. Allow to dry thoroughly. Remove tear-away stabilizer from back of fence. Using appliqué scissors, carefully cut organza away between fence posts. Complete jumper according to pattern directions.

CHAPTER 5

CHAMBRAY SHIRT

YOU WILL NEED:

- Button covers to be used as design
- Scanner paper and black marker
- Scanner
- Embroidery card
- Chambray shirt
- Adhesive-backed stabilizer
- Water-soluble marker
- Rayon thread

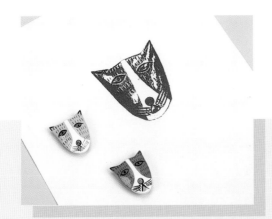

1. Enlarge button cover design to desired size on photocopier. Place a piece of scanning paper over copied button cover design. Design must fit within the scanable area of the paper. Trace copied motif onto scanner paper using black marker.

2. Run scanner over motif. Repeat the process for each color in the motif following the directions for your particular scanner. When scanning is complete, save motif on an embroidery card.

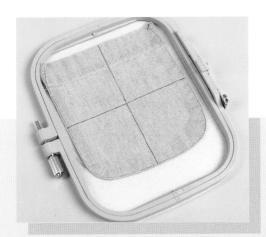

3. Remove pocket from shirt and draw horizontal and vertical placement lines on pocket. Place adhesive-backed stabilizer or Hoop-it-All to wrong side of embroidery hoop and place pocket in hoop matching lines on pocket with lines on hoop.

4. Insert embroidery card into machine and select motif. Stitch motif and remove pocket from hoop. Stitch pocket to shirt.

"FANTASEA" EVENING GOWN

(PFAFF)

YOU WILL NEED:

- Scanner paper and black marker
- Scanner
- Evening gown pattern of choice

- Sueded silk fabric
- Dressmaker's pencil
- Rayon thread
- Tear-away stabilizer
- Fabric stiffener (light)
- Coordinating cords and braids

- Braiding/couching foot
- Monofilament thread
- Seam sealant
- Water-soluble or heat-away stabilizer
- Fabric glue stick
- Austrian crystals

1. Create border waves by scanning your original design using the Pfaff "Fill-in Option A". Cut gown from sueded silk fabric. Make a template of your design and use this template to mark the desired placement of the waves on the pattern pieces. Mark horizontal and vertical placement lines and center. Embroider motifs on stabilized fabric.

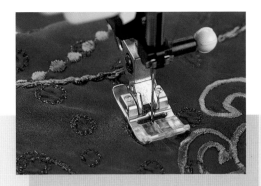

2. To create a "bubble" design across the bodice of the gown and along the slit, select stitch #150 and stitch in a variety of sizes. Note: Use fabric stiffener where necessary to stabilize fabric. Test on remnant first to avoid spotting.

3. Groups of the same cords, braids and threads used in the embroidery are twisted together, threaded through the metal loop on the front of the braiding foot and couched to the design. Stitch over the cord with a monofilament thread.

4. To create free-flowing fins, embroider all fins; apply seam sealant around outer edges. Trim close to stitching. Mark placement, layer water-soluble stabilizer and fabric in hoop, and embroider colors to create fish. Glue fins in place; complete fish embroidery by adding Austrian crystals.

Monogrammed Clutch

- Dressmaker's pencil
- 2 - 11" x 12" pieces of velvet
- Adhesive-backed stabilizer
- Rayon thread
- 3/4 yard narrow decorative cording
- 2 - 11" x 12" pieces of lining
- Needle and thread

1. Mark placement line for monogram on right side of fabric using a dressmaker's pencil (test pencil on scrap of fabric to be sure markings are easily removed). Follow directions in the instruction manual for your machine regarding the correct placement of letters for monogramming.

2. Place adhesive-backed stabilizer on underside of the embroidery hoop or use Hoop-it-All. Place velvet, wrong side down, matching marked lines on fabric with marks on hoop. Program monogram and stitch. Note: Make sure the bottom of letters face edge of fabric closest to marked line.

3. Stitch front and back of clutch, right sides together, along bottom and side edges. Baste decorative cord to top edge of clutch keeping edge of cord even with raw edge of clutch.

4. Stitch lining pieces, right side together, along side edges. Stitch along bottom edge leaving a 4" opening in center of seam. Stitch clutch and lining, right sides together, along top edge. Turn right side out through opening in lining. Slipstitch opening closed with needle and thread.

$\mathscr{M}$ONOGRAMMED $\mathscr{S}$CARF

YOU WILL NEED:

- 51" x 9" piece of black wool crepe
- Dressmaker's pencil
- Tear-away stabilizer

- Rayon thread and black metallic thread to match reverse side of scarf
- Contrasting fabric for reverse side of scarf (same measurements)

- Water-soluble marker
- Iron-on stabilizer
- Needle and thread

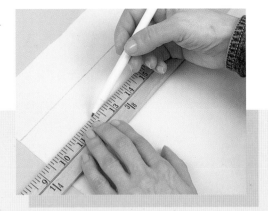

1. Place black fabric around your shoulders. With a dressmaker's pencil, mark side on right with an "R" and side on left with an "L". Draw a horizontal line 5" from each short edge of scarf. Draw a vertical line in center of scarf from short edges through horizontal line. Using tear-away stabilizer, stabilize and hoop fabric, matching lines with marks on hoop. Stitch initial of first name on side of scarf marked "R" and initial of last name on side of the scarf marked "L".

2. Using a water-soluble marker, mark a horizontal line along short edges of contrasting fabric 1" from short edge. Draw two additional lines 2" and 3" from short edge. Fuse stabilizer to wrong side of contrasting fabric at marked lines.

3. Stitch row of large decorative stitching between center line and lower line. Mirror-image stitch and repeat between center and upper lines. Stitch scarf front to scarf back, right sides together, leaving an opening in one long edge for turning. Turn scarf right side out; slip-stitch opening closed with needle and thread.

DINOSAUR BACKPACK

(BROTHER INTERNATIONAL CORP.)

YOU WILL NEED:

- Brother Embroidery Cards - #3,#5, and #7
- McCall's #803/6320 or appropriate pattern
- Fabric and notions as required on pattern
- Solid fabric for flap
- Tear-away stabilizer
- Rayon thread in greens and earth tones
- Water-soluble marker
- 1 package iron-on vinyl fabric coating

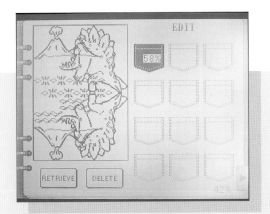

1. Refer to your Pacesetter PC-8200 manual to become familiar with the editing mode. To create design: a) select dinosaur and move image to upper right; b) select same dinosaur, mirror-image the motif, turn it 90°, and move to right; c) select volcano and move to left; d) select same volcano, mirror-image, rotate 90°, and move to left; e) without turning off machine, remove card #3 and insert card #7, select grass and move so tufts of grass are in upper left of screen, select grass a second time and move so it is opposite first grass pattern; e) remove card #7 and insert card #5, select water sign and move water to the bottom half of screen, select water a second time and place it at lower dinosaur's feet; f) select end edit to save scene.

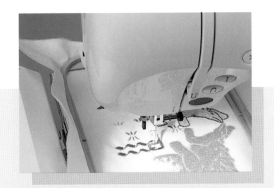

2. Place stabilized flap fabric in center of hoop. When stitching scene, stop sewing when first volcano tapers to point on dinosaur's right side. Forward through second volcano until outline stitching is reached. Begin sewing. Repeat procedure with "reflected" volcano. When stitching grass, forward to skip diamond shapes between grass tufts.

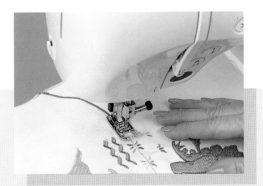

3. Remove fabric from hoop. Draw a line between top and bottom scenes and draw three semi-circles at nose of top dinosaur. Stitch along marked lines with a satin stitch. Laminate fabric according to manufacturer's directions. Cut out flap and construct backpack and flap according to pattern directions.

CHRISTMAS APRON

(BROTHER INTERNATIONAL CORP.)

YOU WILL NEED:

- Paper-backed fusible web
- 12" x 9" remnant for house
- Purchased or sewn green chef's apron
- Metallic thread
- Brother Embroidery Card #8
- Rayon thread
- 13" x 6" remnant for roof
- 3" x 2" remnant for chimney
- Dressmaker's pencil
- Tear-away stabilizer

1. Press fusible web to wrong side of house fabric. Trim 1/2" from each edge of fabric. Remove paper backing and fuse house to apron. Mark placement of door and window, stitch over marked lines with a satin stitch. Using embroidery card, stitch wreath on door and Christmas tree in the window.

2. Press fusible web to wrong side of roof and chimney fabrics. Trim 1/2" from each edge, remove paper backing and fuse in place. Satin-stitch around the edges of the roof. Mark placement of Santa on top of the roof. Center placement lines in embroidery hoop and back fabric with tear-away stabilizer. Stitch Santa motif with rayon thread.

3. With fabric in large hoop, randomly embroider snowflakes above and around house. Select snowflake motif and move motif to desired position within the hoop. When embroidery is complete, move the hoop again and stitch another motif. Place fabric in hoop again and stitch snowflakes as desired.

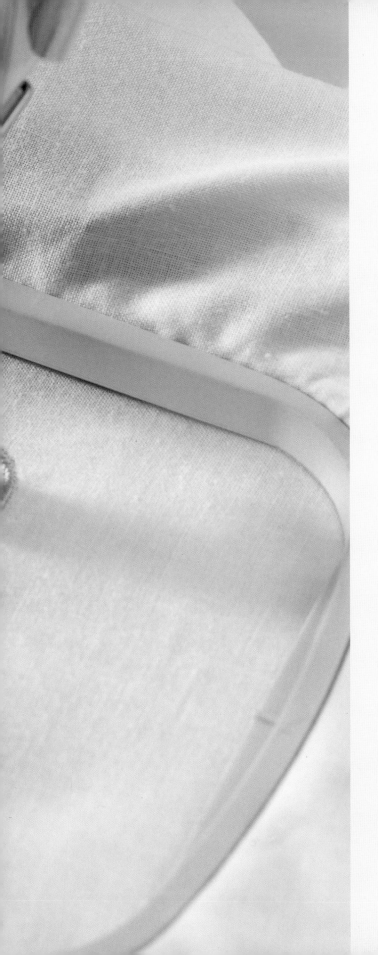

GIFT IDEAS

The perfect gift for any
occasion can be easily created with
an embroidery motif. Turn basic
sheets and towels into a favorite
housewarming gift by embellishing
with a special embroidery. Or create
the perfect table ensemble with
coordinated napkins and place mats.
A simple pillow becomes an elegant
gift with the added touch of cutwork.
Commemorate a special anniversary
or the birth of a child with a
wonderful wall hanging or adorable
personalized pillowcases

Anniversary Wall Hanging

YOU WILL NEED:

- Water-soluble marker
- 4 - 12" x 12" pieces of white fabric
- Tear-away stabilizer
- Rayon thread in a variety of colors
- Gold metallic thread
- Ruler
- 5 - 8" x 4" pieces of calico
- 2 - 51" x 4" strips of calico fabric
- 1 - 51" x 16" piece of fusible batting
- 1 - 51" x 16" piece of calico
- 2 packages of extra-wide double-fold bias tape

1. Draw horizontal and vertical lines in center of each white square. Place stabilized fabric in embroidery hoop, matching markings on hoop with lines on fabric. Horizontal line on fabric should match middle hoop marking. Stitch desired motif in upper section of hoop. Reposition hoop and embroider appropriate year or date with metallic thread. Repeat with remaining squares.

2. Remove stabilizer from back of embroidery. Draw a line 2" from each edge of embroidered square. Trim along marked lines to create 8" squares.

3. Using 8" x 4" bands of fabric, stitch a band to top and bottom of each embroidery to create one long piece of fabric. Stitch long calico strips to each side of center panel.

4. Fuse batting to wrong side of wall hanging. Baste calico lining to wall hanging, wrong sides together. Encase raw edges of wall hanging with bias tape.

EMBROIDERED TOWELS

YOU WILL NEED:

- Bath towel
- Water-soluble marker
- Water-soluble stabilizer
- Tear-away stabilizer
- Rayon thread in assorted colors

- 1/4 yard coordinating fabric
- 3/4 yard of 1"-wide ribbon

1. Mark desired placement of embroidery on front of towel. Place towel in embroidery hoop with water-soluble stabilizer on top and tear-away stabilizer on bottom. Embroider desired motif. Remove stabilizer, rinsing away excess stabilizer under cool water.

2. To make ruffle, cut a 4" strip of fabric twice the width of towel. Finish the two short ends of the strip and one long edge with a rolled hem edge finish on the serger. Gather the opposite edge on the serger or sewing machine.

3. Baste ruffle to towel, keeping bottom of ruffle even with bottom of towel. Center ribbon over raw edge of ruffle. Turn under 1/4" at each end of ribbon and stitch in place close to edges of ribbon.

BABY PILLOWCASE

(BERNINA OF AMERICA)

YOU WILL NEED:

- Water-soluble marker
- Ruler
- Purchased pillowcases
- Tear-away stabilizer
- Rayon thread

1. Using a water-soluble marker, mark placement line for name on front of pillowcase about 6" from finished edge. Open side and seams of pillowcase.

2. Program desired name into sewing machine. Stitch a test sample to see which direction the name is sewn as it may be necessary to rotate name before stitching. Stabilize and hoop fabric; stitch name.

3. Mark placement line for center motif at top of pillowcase. Stabilize and hoop fabric. Select motif, rotate, and reposition as necessary. Repeat with remaining motifs. When you have finished the embroideries, stitch the pillowcase together along seams, using a serger.

Boudoir Pillow

(BERNINA)

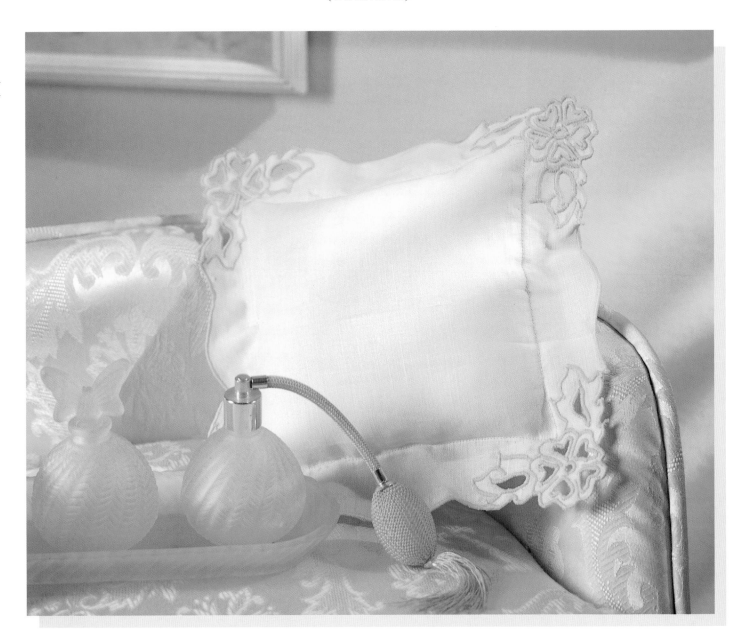

YOU WILL NEED:

- 1/2 yard linen
- Disappearing marker
- Scanning paper and black marker
- Scanner
- Embroidery card
- Water-soluble stabilizer
- 2 spools of polyester thread
- Fiber Etch™ fabric remover
- Polyester fiberfill

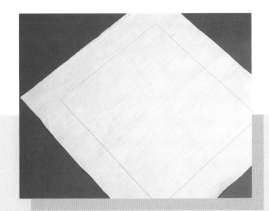

1. Cut a 16" square for the pillow top. Using a disappearing marker, center and trace a 12" square on pillow front. Machine baste along marked lines.

2. Trace and scan cutwork design. Save motif on embroidery card and insert into machine. Sandwich fabric between layers of water-soluble stabilizer. Center one corner of pillow in embroidery hoop and stitch motif. Repeat on remaining three corners.

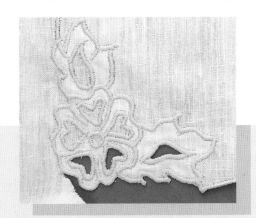

3. Remove stabilizer. Satin-stitch along each edge to connect motifs. Apply Fiber Etch to inner floral and petal areas and to outside edge of embroidery. Allow to dry completely. From wrong side, press etched areas with hot iron. Gently pull away excess fabric when treated area begins to turn brown.

4. To complete pillow, cut a square of fabric 1 1/2" smaller than pillow front. Turn and press under 1/2" on all sides of square. Center this square on back of pillow front. Stitch close to fold on three sides. Stuff pillow with fiberfill and stitch remaining side on sewing machine.

NAPKINS AND PLACE MATS

(SINGER)

YOU WILL NEED:

- Scanning paper and black marker
- Scanner
- Embroidery card
- 2 yards linen-like fabric
- Water-soluble marker

- Tear-away stabilizer
- Rayon thread
- Contrasting fabric for place mat trim
- Optional: textured nylon thread

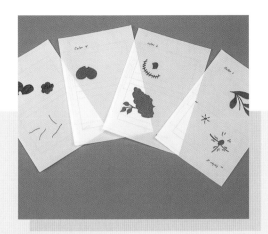

1. Draw or trace floral motif onto scanning paper using a black marker. You will need a separate drawing for each color in motif. Note: Refer to your instruction manual for complete scanning directions.

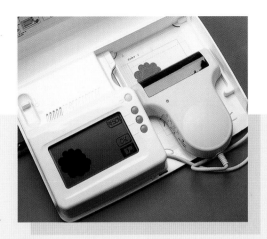

2. Beginning with first color, run scanner over each section of design. After all colors have been scanned, save motif on an embroidery card.

3. Cut desired size napkin and place mats from linen fabric. Mark placement of embroidery on each place mat and napkin with a water-soluble marker. Place stabilized fabric in hoop. Insert embroidery card into machine; select motif.

4. Stitch floral motif on each napkin and place mat. Trim edges of place mats with a contrasting fabric band. Edges of napkins may be finished with a rolled hem using a textured nylon thread.

EMBROIDERED *S*HEETS AND *P*ILLOWCASE

YOU WILL NEED:

- Template marker
- Purchased sheets and pillowcase
- Template grid
- Water-soluble marker
- Adhesive-backed stabilizer
- Iron-on stabilizer
- Rayon thread in assorted colors

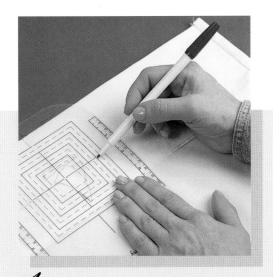

1. Stitch sample motif on scrap of fabric. Trace motif onto template grid. Mark placement of motif along top edge of sheet and hem of pillowcase with water-soluble marker. Note: Embroidery must be sewn upside down, so when sheet is turned down the embroidery is upright.

2. Place adhesive-backed stabilizer on underside of hoop, adhesive side up. Place wrong side of sheet on stabilizer, matching placement lines with markings on hoop. Select motif, rotate twice (design is upside down) and stitch. Stitch additional motifs on markings. Remove sheet from hoop.

3. Draw a line parallel to bottom edge of motifs. Fuse stabilizer to wrong side of sheet and pillowcase edges. Select appropriate decorative stitch and sew along marked line. Remove stabilizer and remove marked line with cool water.

Baby Bib Pattern - Page 58

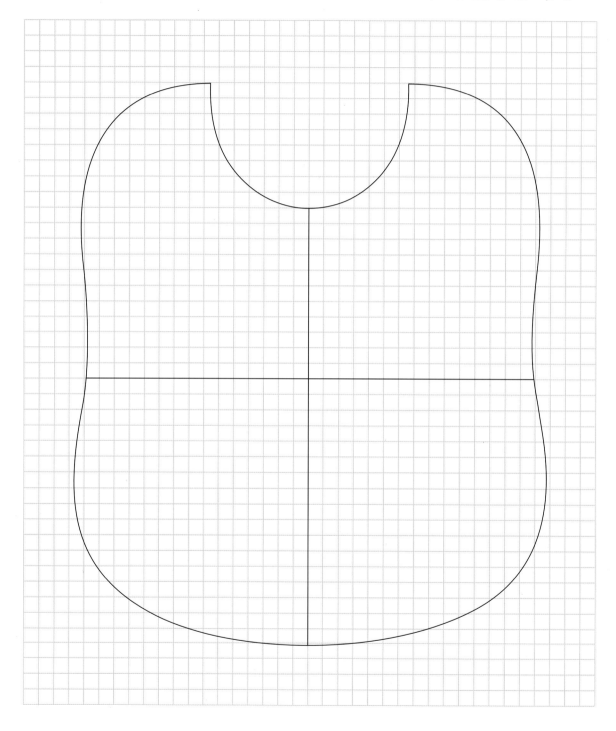

Greeting Cards Template - Page 68

Silver Server Pattern - PAGE 64

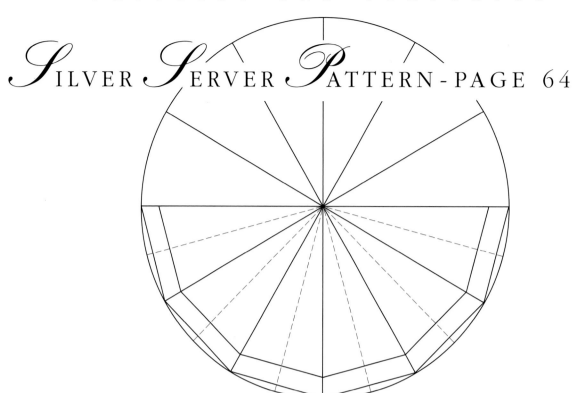

Peter Rabbit Valance Pattern - PAGE 82

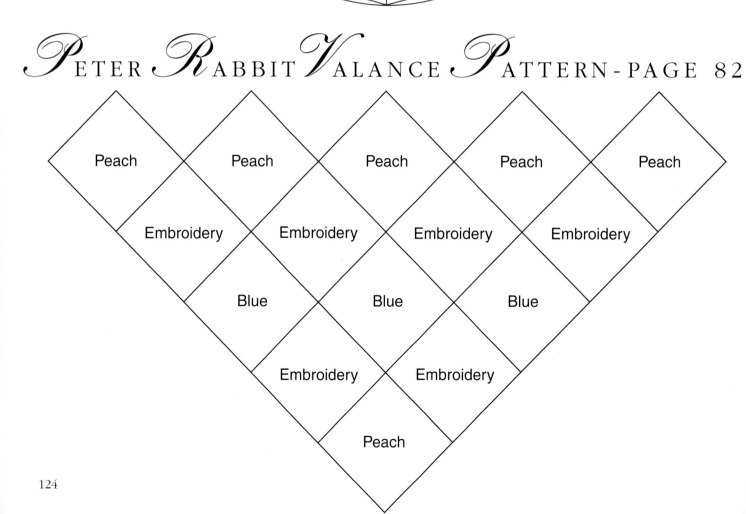

ACKNOWLEDGMENTS

To Bernina of America, New Home Sewing Machine Company, and Singer Sewing Company for providing sewing equipment, information, and projects.

To Laura Haynie of Pfaff American Sales for providing sewing product, extra projects, and assistance with photography.

To Nancy Jewell of Husqvarna Viking and June Mellinger of Brother International Corporation for sending me whatever I asked for at the last minute along with sewing product and projects. Special thanks to June for coming into New York twice to help out with photography.

To the following companies for providing notions and supplies: Dritz, Handler Textiles, Sulky of America, Coats & Clark, Hoop-it-All, and SCS Distributors.

To Trish Buczek of Royce Sewing Center for providing me with embroidery cards and props.

To Karen Kunkel Schaphorst for providing me with additional information on scanners and embroidery machines.

To JoAnn Pugh-Gannon for giving me the opportunity to finally write my own book, along with her encouragement and helpful hints.

To Barbara Cornea and Patty Jo Larson for their sewing assistance — I could not have completed all my projects without them!

CREDITS

Projects provided by sewing machine companies were created by the following sewing experts:

Nancy Bednar, Bernina of America -
 Boudoir Pillow, page 116.

Didi Gerhold, Brother International Corp. -
 Dinosaur Backpack, page 104.

Kim Fillmore, Pfaff American Sales Corp. -
 "Fantasea" Evening Gown, page 98.

Christine Halik, Pfaff American Sales Corp. -
 Silver Server, page 64.
 Table Runner, page 66.
 Embroidered Table Topper, page 90.
 Picture Frame, page 88.

Laura Haynie, Pfaff American Sales Corp. -
 Lampshade, page 86.

Patty Jo Larson, Husqvarna Viking -
 Heirloom Pillow, page 84.
 Picket Fence Dress, page 94.

Agnes Mercik, Bernina of America -
 Baby Pillowcase, page 114.

Janice Pfeiffenberger, Brother International Corp. -
 Christmas Apron, page 106.

Singer Sewing Company -
 Bridal Album Cover, page 62.
 Napkins and Place Mats, page 118.